Little Laureates

Yorkshire Voices
Edited by Angela Fairbrace

Young Writers

First published in Great Britain in 2007 by:
Young Writers
Remus House
Coltsfoot Drive
Peterborough
PE2 9JX
Telephone: 01733 890066
Website: www.youngwriters.co.uk

SB ISBN 978-1 84431 168 2

Foreword

Young Writers was established in 1991 and has been passionately devoted to the promotion of reading and writing in children and young adults ever since. The quest continues today. Young Writers remains as committed to the nurturing of poetic and literary talent as ever.

This year's Young Writers competition has proven as vibrant and dynamic as ever and we are delighted to present a showcase of the best poetry from across the UK and in some cases overseas. Each poem has been selected from a wealth of *Little Laureates* entries before ultimately being published in this, our sixteenth primary school poetry series.

Once again, we have been supremely impressed by the overall quality of the entries we have received. The imagination, energy and creativity which has gone into each young writer's entry made choosing the poems a challenging and often difficult but ultimately hugely rewarding task - the general high standard of the work submitted ensured this opportunity to bring their poetry to a larger appreciative audience.

We sincerely hope you are pleased with this final collection and that you will enjoy *Little Laureates Yorkshire Voices* for many years to come.

Contents

Bronach Kelly (9)	16
Charlotte Mawson (9)	17
Will Medd (8)	17
Freddy Webster (8)	18
Bradley Rawling (9)	18
Lydia Cunniffe (9)	19
Megan Farrington (8)	19
Bryony Curtis (9)	20
Aled Vernon-Rees (8)	20
Chloe North (8)	20
Alice Burley (9)	21
Aaron Acaster (8)	21
Hannah Stones (8)	21
Josh Kwiatkowski (9)	22
Simon Coning (8)	22

Gilberdyke Primary School

Shelby Walton (8)	22
Katy Robinson (8)	23
Rebecca Leeman (8)	23
Emily Abba (9)	24
Jessica Lister (11)	24
James Bently Williamson (11)	25
Louise Brown (9)	25
Lorna Whur (10)	26
Natalie Marie White (10)	26
Sarah Barrett (11)	27
Laura Ward (10)	27
Christopher Laws (10)	28
Matthew White (10)	28
Chloe Walker (9)	29
Michelle Brown (7)	29
Sam Barnes (9)	30
Ashley Thomas Holt (8)	30
Callum West (10)	31
Bethany Whur (8)	31
Sophie Williamson (10)	32
Leah Davy (8)	32
Jessica Marrison (11)	33
Georgina Ibbotson (10)	33
Sophie Bielby (10)	34

Rebekah Kay Woodward (9)	34
Laura Sims (10)	35
Eleanor Bielby (8)	35
Paris Louise Share (10)	36
James Whitton (8)	36
Tom Collins (10)	37
Sky Duke (7)	37
Ted Sefton (10)	38
Louis Turner (11)	38
Olivia Maddison (7)	39
Amelia Marrison (8)	39
Chelsea Sharman (8)	40
Elliott Stone (7)	40
Chloe Bentley (8)	41
Connor Luke Dobson (8)	41
Toby Conboy (10)	42
Adam Salisbury (8)	42
Harry Roy Walker (11)	43
Rebecca Routledge (7)	43
Stephanie Whitton (10)	44
Andrew Winchester (7)	44
Abigail Ibbotson (9)	45
Aimee Gregson (7)	45
Daniel David Routledge (10)	46
Emma Holt (10)	46
Keeley Mogg (11)	47
Daniel Fozard (9)	47
Bronwen Alice Hall (10)	48
Christopher Jackson (11)	48
Amy Norton (10)	49
Bethany Share (9)	49
Kelly Huby (10)	50
Daniel Shaw (9)	50
Scott Davy (11)	51
Joe Sefton (9)	51
Ben Lister (10)	52
Devon Thompson (9)	53
James Barnes (11)	54
Benjamin Kitching (10)	55
Beth Dredge (9)	56
Shannon Lucy Rastrick (8)	56
Katie Louise Last (8)	57

Megan Malcolmson (9)	57
Lauren Champion (9)	58
Jack Copley (8)	58
Amanda Winchester (9)	59

Hornsea Community Primary School

Ryan Thorne (10)	59
Tyler Fletcher (10)	60
Maddie Walton (10)	60
Megan Gell (10)	61
George Anthony (11)	61
Olivia Clubley (10)	62
Adam Bodsworth (10)	62
Josh Cooper (10)	63
Lucy Bell (11)	63
Joseph Whincup (11)	64
Adam Railton (11)	64
Dan Wilkinson (10)	65
Thomas Catley (11)	65
Ellie Senior-Farmer (10)	66
Kieran Baines (10)	67
Sadie Dickson (11)	68
Laura Smith (11)	68
Liam Moffat (10)	69
Josh Beck (11)	69
Jasmin Dearing (10)	70
Brooke Knight (11)	70
Matthew Sinar (10)	71
Katy Brooks (11)	71
Liam Tudor-Bateman (11)	72
Jessica Beevers (11)	72
Holly Brown (11)	73
Amy Jenney (11)	73
Amber Softley (11)	74
Emily Williams (11)	75
Tessa Watson (10)	76
Jack Shepherd (11)	76
Libby Wallwork (10)	77
James Oliphant (10)	77
Ben McGill (10)	78
Deanna Postill (10)	78

Daniel Ellmer (11)	79
Ashleigh Metcalf (10)	79
Charlie Kelly (10)	80
James Osborne (10)	81
Chloe Fitzgerald (11)	82
Tom Duckworth (11)	83
Adam Yorke (11)	84
Lewis Wood (11)	84
Jay Vaughan (11)	85
Peter Simms (10)	85
Jacob Richards (10)	86
Charlie Stork (10)	86
Amy Sinar (10)	87
Ben Samuel (11)	87
Craig Monkman (10)	88
Abigail Abey (11)	88
Viki Henderson (11)	89
Jordan Hillerby (11)	89
Danielle Sullivan (11)	90
Hannah Marsh (10)	91
Danielle Gray (10)	92
Dominic Edwards (10)	93
Shelley Francis (10)	94
Haden Holmes (11)	95
Jessica Acklam (11)	96
Mark Williams (11)	97
Zara-Faith Evans (10)	98
Jack Tonks (10)	99

Longman's Hill CP School

Emma Pilling (10)	100
Patrick Gouldsbrough (10)	100
Ben Pike (10)	101
Angus Kirkby (10)	101
Jake Holliday (10)	102
Stuart Fox (11)	102
Liam O'Hara (10)	103
Josh Pike (10)	103
Lewis Connell (11)	104
Oliver Bloxham (10)	104
Georgia Southern (10)	105

Kacey Sorby Richardson (11)	105
Jack Noble (11)	106
Mark Heslam (10)	106
Jennifer Wilson (10)	107
Bethany Stephenson (11)	107
Tom Bruce (11)	108
Liam Golton (11)	109
Courtney Eleanor Render (10)	110
Billy Glassby (11)	110
Grace Dowdy (10)	111
Evie Smyth (11)	111
Lucy Crawford (9)	112
Connor Mumby (11)	112
Sam Hawe (11)	113
Matthew O'Connor (10)	113
Katie May Todd (11)	114
Ellis Piercy (11)	115
Robert Howard (11)	116

Sidmouth Primary School

Jasmine Ruby Hale (9)	117
Alisha Freer (9)	117
Lewis Alex Scott (8)	118
Molly Wagner (8)	118
Yasmin Malek (9)	118

Southcoates Primary School

Ross Cudbertson (9)	119
Courtney Wilson (9)	119

Sutton Park Primary School

Saffie Pick (9)	120

The Poems

Seasons - Haikus

Winter waves:

As sad as grey waves
Waves crashing strongly, windy
Winter is coming.

Summer sun:

Happy sun smiling,
Flowers in a bright green field
Colours everywhere.

Alex Giblin (9)
Cavendish Primary School

Seasons

Sad winter waves
Crashing by the rocks
Bang, bang, crash, winter waves.

Happy flower days
Walking in a field
Summer days, summer days,
In a flower field.

Joseph Hildreth (9)
Cavendish Primary School

Sea In Peril - Haiku

Crashing waves around
Making loud thundery sounds
Purple, blue, black skies.

Max Cheesbrough (9)
Cavendish Primary School

Seasons

The horrible ocean:

Sad winter waves, horrible,
Crashing around like an angry elephant,
Foamy, heavy and windy
Like the world falling apart.

Happy flowers:

Flower times, lots of nice colours,
Fine, nice breeze, flowers swaying,
Children running around on the grass.

Callum James Howard (8)
Cavendish Primary School

Seasons

Winter sea:

Morning winter sea
Waves crashing on rocks
Winter is cold.

Happy holidays:

Happy flowers, summery
Little dancing flowers
Summer is hot.

Harry Hudson (9)
Cavendish Primary School

Seasons

Winter waves:

Feel sad when waves are strong
and frost covers the land.
Falling water falls
making light currents.

Sunny weather:

Feeling happy in meadows
flowers colourful, bright and fresh.
Summer is here
a new start.

Brooke Sunlay (8)
Cavendish Primary School

Weather - Haikus

Stormy seas:

Crashing waves, dark sky
Winter weather now coming
Horrible and dull.

Summer sun:

Summer everywhere
A sunny day with flowers
Bright colours, green grass.

Aimee Feetham (8)
Cavendish Primary School

Seasons

Sad splashes:

Sad like the seaside
Waves falling, crashing
Into the wintry, watery depths.

Breezy winds:

Golden fields swaying in the breeze
Flowers happy like the sun
Rabbits hopping, bees landing, birds singing
And having fun.

Jez Cooney (8)
Cavendish Primary School

Dog

Fluffy white ball of fluff
Runs about in the mud
Waggy tail, tongue of wet
Barks, jumps, messes about
Makes me feel really happy.

Chanel Hall (8)
Dorchester Primary School

Monkey

Orange and browny hair.
Like a scary gorilla.
Always happy, smiley and funny.
Makes me laugh.

Tyrone Warhurst (8)
Dorchester Primary School

Dog

It's black and grey and brown
It runs and jumps and chews a bone
It makes me happy
It is fluffy
It is big
It is round like a ball
It makes me laugh and smile
It is thoughtful and kind.

Chloe Chapman (7)
Dorchester Primary School

Dog

I am a dog that runs for its tail
and barks all day.

I am a dog that goes to sleep
and sleeps all day.

That makes me feel like a happy chappy.

Thalia Slade (7)
Dorchester Primary School

Fox

Comes out at night.
Runs for his life.
Pointed ears.
Gets his food from dustbins.
Sneaks so no one can see him.
Howls as well.
He is red, white and orange.

Amber Sanderson (7)
Dorchester Primary School

Giraffe

Very long indeed.
It is very spotty, brown and yellow
It reaches when it is hungry to eat
It is always cheeky and it gobbles
It makes me feel excited, happy and jealous
Because it has a long neck and I don't!

Sophie Wright (7)
Dorchester Primary School

Dolphin

Big and blue and slimy too
Slithers like a lizard
Splashes! What a naughty thing to do, don't you think?
Light blue animal that is blue like the sea
Makes me feel happy.

Jordan Clark (7)
Dorchester Primary School

Monkey

Smooth, hairy little monkey.
Jumps off trees.
Looks like a little hairy gorilla.
Climbs, sleeps upon the leaves.

Charlotte Whittles (7)
Dorchester Primary School

Friends

Friends are for everyone
Friends are everywhere
Friends are in your heart
And they will always be there

Friends are like family
Heart to heart
Friends always care
Heart to heart

Friends are in your classroom
Friends are at your home
Friends are at dance class
Friends are at football too

Friends are like passion
Passion to always care
Friends are for life
Friends are everywhere.

Chloe Jade Bailey (10)
Eastfield Primary School

Dragons

Magical creatures are ace,
But dragons are best by far,
Loads of different colours and strengths,
And larger than a star.

With fire-proof reptilian scales,
And wings of adamantium,
I think dragons are ace,
Don't you?

Joshua Burnett (10)
Eastfield Primary School

Seasons

Spring fades in our lives
With a fresh intention
Flowers are everywhere
It's a good sensation!

Summer's finally here
So we'll go to the beach!
The weather's fantastic
The sun is like a peach.

Autumn's when the leaves fall
The trees are all so bare
Brown leaves are all we find
It's so muddy . . . *not fair!*

Winter is all so white
It's like a snow blanket
The atmosphere is cold
Winter just doesn't fit!

Spring fades in our lives
With a fresh intention
Flowers are everywhere
It's a good sensation!

Sarwat Malik (11)
Eastfield Primary School

The Tiger

In the lush tropical forest,
Lives the sneaky tiger,
Rain or sun never matters to him,
Snowy storms come across his path.

His stripes of dark,
His skin of bright,
His ears made to harken,
His eyes reflect the silver moonlight.

The sun rises,
In the dozing mountains,
Waiting for the classic roar
Of the dreaded tiger in the fresh crisp air.

His claws like talons,
His nose so wet,
His tongue sloppy with saliva,
His tail never calm . . .

But he is the prince, the prince of the jungle.

Lily Blount (10)
Eastfield Primary School

The Solar System

The solar system is immense
Eight planets surround
Though none as large as the sun
The solar system is immense

The solar system is colossal
Meteors all around
Though none as big as Saturn
The solar system is colossal

The solar system is immeasurable
Our Earth is tiny in comparison
Though not as small as Mars
The solar system is immeasurable

The solar system is superb
It's around the sun
Though it's not the biggest star
The solar system is superb

The solar system is immense
Eight planets surround
Though none as big as Jupiter
The solar system is immense.

Connor Mennell (10)
Eastfield Primary School

Come On FC!

Come on FC, come on FC!
You can do it!
Just one more try
And you'll be ahead by a bit!

Come on FC, come on FC!
We're cheering for you,
We think you can win
And you should too!

Come on FC, come on FC!
We're sure you can win,
So put these Rhinos
In the bin!

Come on FC, come on FC!
Not long to go,
You're eighteen-six up
And running the show!

Yeess!
Well done FC, well done FC!
You won the game,
Isn't it a pity
The Leeds' fans came?

Sam Poppleton (11)
Eastfield Primary School

My House

My house is very pretty and cool
it's there when I come home from school,
the grass is green,
the trees are tall,
I do hope they don't get blown over or fall.

But in the night when I go to bed,
I dream about it in my head,
It has a door for a mouth,
Windows for eyes,
Sometimes I don't understand why, oh why?

So that's my house, now don't you see?
Would you like to come with me?

Georgia Wilson (10)
Eastfield Primary School

My Family

My brother's very small,
My sister's quite tall,
My mum is kind of mad
And so is my dad.

My cousin's always sharing,
My auntie's always caring,
My uncle's always funny,
My nana's short of money.

Now that you've met my family,
You would think that they're alright,
Even though I think they're crazy,
I've loved them all my life.

Evie Collier (11)
Eastfield Primary School

The Chocolate Room!

The chocolate room is made of sweets.
Big ones, small ones,
Round ones, square ones,
Soft ones, hard ones, oh, what big treats!

Trees of candyfloss and snakes of cola laces,
There's a waterfall of chocolate,
Come on, let's stuff our faces!

Let's go on a boat ride on the chocolate stream,
And eat at the sides,
See clouds of whipped cream!

Now we have to sleep and rest our heads on candyfloss pillows,
Let us sleep in the land of sherbet saucers,
And leave the room made of chocolate . . .

So sleep tight and mind the liquorice ants don't wriggle
into your mouths!

Jasmine Langcaster-James (11)
Eastfield Primary School

My Mum

My mum is passionate
My mum is sweet
Ask for something
She will repeat.

Give her kisses all day long
She makes us eat healthy food
She can't stand it when we are rude.

When she kisses me outside school
It makes me look like a big fool
Apart from that she's really cool!

Jessica Rose Winduss (11)
Eastfield Primary School

The Soldier

The soldier is young and eager, only seventeen,
Willing to risk his life for victory for his country.

He fights and fights,
Day and night,
Hoping to come back alive,

Or be remembered for bravery and courage,
Then when he's dead and gone,
And tears flood the land,
His memory will live on.

Rosy Leech (9)
Forest of Galtres School

D-Day

Mighty D-Day,
To take back France,
Our beloved friend,
Mighty D-Day,
Mighty D-Day.

Powerful Germany buckles
In its defences,
To keep France,
Mighty D-Day,
Mighty D-Day!

Every day they slowly advance,
Confident for victory,
Mighty D-Day,
Mighty D-Day!

Callum Jackson (9)
Forest of Galtres School

The Inferno Bird

The inferno bird is a boiling spark,
Twisting, diving for his prey,
Spinning in the distance,
Waiting patiently for his prey.

He glides like a plane,
Feathers falling like colourful parachutes.
Then he discontinues his hunt,
He swoops down for the execution of his prey,
Like a man with a dagger.

Chris Scurr (9)
Forest of Galtres School

The Blitz

Planes flying,
People crying,
Adults shouting,
Babies whining,
Doors shutting,
Locks locking,
Look out, there's
A plane flying!
Dogs barking,
Rabbits running,
Bombs dropping,
Like water balloons,
Bang! Bang!
              Duck!

Ella
Forest of Galtres School

France

France,
Is a cool place.
Lots of different foods to try,
Like snails, eclairs and wine.
Munch, munch, munch, munch!

France,
Has lots of places to go,
Like La Rochelle and Paris.
There are also lots of tracks for bikers,
Pedal, pedal, pedal, pedal!

France,
Has a different language from us,
They speak really fast,
So it's really hard work to understand,
Chat, chat, chat, chat!

Au revoir.

Verity Ellis (9)
Forest of Galtres School

The Snow

The snow is like
Petals from a cherry blossom tree,
Falling onto my face,
It turns and swirls around and around,
Then up comes the big sun,
And the little snow goes away,
And then I wait another day.

Bronach Kelly (9)
Forest of Galtres School

Moaning Minnie

All is soundless
When we're asleep, asleep,
Asleep.
But suddenly Moaning Minnie,
Is starting,
Starting, starting!
The sound it's making
Is like a siren going round and round
Boom! Crash!
Moaning Minnie
Has had a visit from
A bomb!
Oh no! Oh no,
No more warning!

Charlotte Mawson (9)
Forest of Galtres School

Bugatti Veron

Its engine goes on and its lights go on.
It accelerates and it's off.
It's a mean, green fighting machine.
The burning tyres rip up the road.
On its first lap it skids and makes a great recovery.
It reaches 253mph.
Stop, stop - finished!

Will Medd (8)
Forest of Galtres School

The Whale

A whale is a blue island,
With a crystal fountain in the centre,
The water reaches out to grab you
Like a swirling hand,
At night he swims down, down, down.

A whale is a blue island,
Big as a giant,
Swiftly swaying through
The gloomy blue sea, sea, sea.

A whale is a blue island,
Bobbing up and down,
Gliding through the waves,
You never want to meet a whale face to face,
Face to face!

Freddy Webster (8)
Forest of Galtres School

The Jaguar

The jaguar is an eagle,
Stalking its prey,
Running in and out of trees,
Quicker than quick,
Faster than fast,
Suddenly it sees an oxen,
It stops,
It crouches down gently,
Through the long reeds and grass,
It pounces with a bite to the throat!

Bradley Rawling (9)
Forest of Galtres School

Best Friends

Best friends are like cuddly teddy bears,
They comfort you.
Nothing like a best friend!

Best friends are like roaring lions,
They stick up for you.
Nothing like a best friend.

Best friends are like sisters and brothers,
They share with you.
Best friends are there for you.
Nothing like a best friend
And there never will be!

Lydia Cunniffe (9)
Forest of Galtres School

The Blitz

All the terror of war
Is creeping up behind me,
The screaming and booming sound,
Dads going out to fight,
Kids scared in the Anderson shelters,
All is silence.
Boom!
Bang!
The sound of Moaning Minnie makes my ears ring, ring!
All is then still.

Megan Farrington (8)
Forest of Galtres School

The Sea

The sea is rough wavy hair,
Rocking from side to side,
It leaps around,
Scattering itself everywhere.
Then!
It splashes its long thick hair,
All over the hot sand.

It drags its wonderful hair,
Back into the water for another day.

Bryony Curtis (9)
Forest of Galtres School

A Monkey

A monkey is a vine
Waving from tree to tree
Rapidly moving like a bird
Collecting peanuts on the way
Aiming to get to its family
Desperate for food
Swing, swing, swing,
Every day.

Aled Vernon-Rees (8)
Forest of Galtres School

Fire

Fire is like a horse's mane
Gliding through the wind.
The fire will demolish everything in its tracks.
It will rip up everything.
When the rain slows, the fire will go out.

Chloe North (8)
Forest of Galtres School

The Penguin

Here is a penguin sitting on an iceberg.
It jumps off into the sea-green water,
It jumps off and spins around like a spinning top,
It waddles side to side,
It lies down and puts its snow blanket on
And nods off back to sleep.

Alice Burley (9)
Forest of Galtres School

Pirates

Pirates are vicious people,
With flags, sculls and crossbones,
With ships as big as whales,
With captains as strong and fierce
As two sharks put together.

Aaron Acaster (8)
Forest of Galtres School

The Weather

The sun is a burning pumpkin,
The rain is a cloud weeping,
The butterfly gliding past
Blends in with the rainbow.

The wind is a hand reaching out
To get you, but as you run away
You see the wind far, far away!

Hannah Stones (8)
Forest of Galtres School

The Lancaster Bomber

The Lancaster bomber
Hurtles through the sky,
Dropping bombs,
Dodging the barrage balloons.
Smoke covering the sky.
Can't see a thing,
Just smoke, smoke, smoke!
I land with one wing, wing, wing!

Josh Kwiatkowski (9)
Forest of Galtres School

Blitz

Blitz, Blitz,
Bombs dropping,
Planes crashing,
People crying,
The smell of petrol,

Blitz! Blitz! Blitz!

Simon Coning (8)
Forest of Galtres School

Shelby

Teeth as white as snow
Lips as pink as a rose
Freckles as brown as a tree
Ears as curly as a snail
Eyelashes as black as a cat
Eyes as blue as the sea
Hair as orange as a tangerine
Nose as pointy as a mountain.

Shelby Walton (8)
Gilberdyke Primary School

Katy

Eyes as blue as the sky.
Teeth like shining crystals.
Hair as yellow as the sun.
Canines as sharp as knives.
Skin as peachy as candy.
Legs as long as one-metre sticks.
Mouth as deep as a swimming pool.
Tongue as long as a tree.
Eyebrows as light as the sun.
Face as pretty as a jewel.
Nose like a rock in the sea.
Freckles as small as an insect.
Ears as soft as velvet.
Lips as red as rubies.
Incisors as sharp as scissors.
Chin as white as snow.
Cheeks as soft as a cat's fur.
Arms as strong as a house.
Nails as sharp as a hedgehog's prickles.
Fingers as long as a tall glass.

Katy Robinson (8)
Gilberdyke Primary School

Rebecca Me

Teeth as white as snow
Freckles as brown as a tree
Eyes as blue as the sea
Nose as pointy as a mini mountain
Ears square like the magic whiteboard
Glasses as green as grass
Hair, blonde like a peach
Mouth, red like a pen.

Rebecca Leeman (8)
Gilberdyke Primary School

Killer Storm - Cinquains

Anxious
Crashing, deep, dull
A flash whirls through the sky
Terrifying and furious
Shocking.

Peaceful
Calm and graceful
Dripping worlds then emerge
Terrific gold sun shimmers bright . . .
Quiet.

Emily Abba (9)
Gilberdyke Primary School

Into The Storm - Cinquains

Silence
Still, motionless
The calm before the storm
Quietly waiting but for what?
Resting.

A crash
A flash of light
Dense clouds, roaring thunder
Glowering skies controlling life
Silence.

Jessica Lister (11)
Gilberdyke Primary School

A Killer Storm - Cinquains

Killer
Life-changing strikes
A death-defying storm
Heaven opens and Hell begins
Shocking

Springtime
All is over
Life emerges again
Squirrels run, a new day's begun
Blue sky.

James Bently Williamson (11)
Gilberdyke Primary School

The Storm And After - Cinquains

Glowing
Terrifying
Clashing, bellowing clouds
Suddenly thunder crashes loud
Panic

Clouds gone
Rainbow shines bright
Thunder's quiet, all's still
Rainbow, rainbow, now you are here
Safe times.

Louise Brown (9)
Gilberdyke Primary School

The Storm And The Calm - Cinquains

Scary
Horrifying
Clashing, bellowing clouds
Lightning-illuminated skies
Finished

Rainbow
Shining above
Arching across the skies
Dewdrops sparkle like butterflies
Happy.

Lorna Whur (10)
Gilberdyke Primary School

The Storm Begins - Cinquains

Bang, crash!
The sky is grey
Lightning strikes up again
Zigzags across the damp, wet sky
Storm gone.

Wake up!
Nature begins
Rainbows are here on time
Birds singing their favourite song
Gorgeous!

Natalie Marie White (10)
Gilberdyke Primary School

Flashing Storm - Cinquains

Rumble
Crashing, crackling
Anxious roaring thunder
Lightning comes, bringing down the sky
Stillness

Quiet
After the storm
Sunny skies coming out
Baby animals being born
It's spring!

Sarah Barrett (11)
Gilberdyke Primary School

The Horrifying Storm - Cinquains

Bang! Crash!
Lightning storms down
Thunder bellows from skies
Horrifying storm rains darkly
Silence

Wake up!
Spring is here now
Everything's bright and clear
My sun is up and here to stay
Shining.

Laura Ward (10)
Gilberdyke Primary School

The Flashing Storm - Cinquains

Bang, crash!
Demanding rain
Hailstone storms rushing in
Lightning flashes across the sky
Zigzags

Quiet
Peaceful sunrise
Gleaming skies start to shine
Anxious skies now filled with beauty
Silence.

Christopher Laws (10)
Gilberdyke Primary School

The Storm Awakens - Cinquains

Pitch-black
Horrifying
Intimidating sky
Lightning illuminates the sky
Finished.

Quiet
Birds start to chirp
Nature's born once again
Gold gleaming sun begins to burn
Silence.

Matthew White (10)
Gilberdyke Primary School

Water Life - Haikus

Sea, so blue and green
Dolphins riding crashing waves
Ginormous whales plunge.

Clouds seem white and grey
Great clouds floating in the sky
Forms rain spitting down.

Rain comes falling down
Makes a colourful rainbow
Taps on the window.

Rivers green and blue
Running through tiny valleys
To the fish it's home.

Sea so blue and green
Dolphins riding crashing waves
Ginormous whales plunge.

Chloe Walker (9)
Gilberdyke Primary School

Michelle

I have skin as pink as a small shell.
I have glasses as red as a beetroot.
I have greeny-grey eyes like the sea.
I have eyelashes the colour of blonde hair.
I have ears like small sweets.
I have a nose like a pointed triangle.
I have hair like a mermaid's.

Michelle Brown (7)
Gilberdyke Primary School

Water Typhoon - Haikus

Crash, bash, goes the sea
Leaping whales plunging high-low
Water on seashore

Mist swirling round trees
Slowly drizzling down a stream
Smog in the distance

Bombardment of hail
Spitting, speeding heavy rain
A showery storm

Current, crashing waves
Streams swishing, swiftly swirling
Racing down the stream

Crash, bash, goes the sea,
Leaping whales plunging high-low
Water on seashore.

Sam Barnes (9)
Gilberdyke Primary School

Ashley

Eyes like the blue sky
Lips like a beautiful tulip
Teeth like a white shark
Tongue as pink as a flower
Canines as sharp as a lion's
Chin like a circle
Cheeks like a rose
Forehead like a soft pillow
Ears like beautiful shells.

Ashley Thomas Holt (8)
Gilberdyke Primary School

Water Cycle - Haikus

Blue ocean sparkles.
Splendid fish swimming slowly.
Speedy sharks darting.

Murky rain in clouds.
Darkening clouds in lightness.
Hostile rain dims light.

Volleying hail drops.
Bombardments of ice on heads.
Showery weather.

Rivers and currents
Reach out into salty seas,
In fluent fast streams.

Blue ocean sparkles
Splendid fish swimming slowly
Speedy sharks darting.

Callum West (10)
Gilberdyke Primary School

Beth

Lips like pink pencils.
Face like a balloon.
Hair brown like a wooden plank.
Nose like a peach.
Mouth like red books.
Ears like curly pasta.

Bethany Whur (8)
Gilberdyke Primary School

The Water Cycle - Haikus

Blue shimmering seas
Colourful fish swirling down
Pretty in bright light

Dark clouds gathering
A ginormous storm breaks out
Rain starts to pour down

It starts to calm down
Rainbows clear the cloudy sky
With a flick of sun

Lakes filling up high
Silent rivers flow to sea
Hurrying onward

Blue shimmering seas
Colourful fish swirling down
Then the stars come out.

Sophie Williamson (10)
Gilberdyke Primary School

Leah

Eyes brown as the bark of a tree.
Mouth as soft as clouds.
Ears as big as an elephant's ears.
Nose as long as an elephant's.
Eyebrows as black as the dark night.
Lips as pink as a rose.
Teeth as white as snow.
Canines as pointed as twigs.
Incisors as sharp as a shark's teeth.
Tongue as long as a ruler.
Chin as hard as a rock.

Leah Davy (8)
Gilberdyke Primary School

The Water Cycle Turns - Haikus

Leaping dolphins splash
As the white-blue tide comes in
Where fish love to swim.

Rivers flow white-blue
Bubbling downstream to the sea
While salt rocks settle

Snow falls down for days
It melts when the sun comes out
Snowmen can be formed

Rain pitter-patters
When rain clouds start to gather
Then water falls down

Leaping dolphins splash
As the white-blue tide comes in
Where fish love to swim.

Jessica Marrison (11)
Gilberdyke Primary School

The Water Cycle Forms - Haikus

Crash, bash, sea meets rocks
Leaping whales dive in and out
All under the stars

Rising up sky-high
Slowly forming haze or fog
White clouds develop

Hail racing to lakes
Rapid rain bucketing down
Slows down to spitting

Rivers, lakes, shape seas
Turning, swirling constantly
Rushing to the sea.

Georgina Ibbotson (10)
Gilberdyke Primary School

Sea Poem - Haikus

Huge whales in the sea.
Whales diving up, plunging down.
People have a swim.

Clouds get very dark,
Soaking up condensation.
People pack away.

Clouds are blown away.
Out pops a dazzling rainbow.
People having fun.

Long rivers flow by,
Passing under stone bridges,
Over waterfalls.

Light, shimmery seas,
Crash on rocks, dazzling drops.
Now it's time for home!

Sophie Bielby (10)
Gilberdyke Primary School

Salty Sea - Haikus

Salty sea so calm
Suddenly plunging dolphins
Splash! They land softly

Crash, thunder, sea rough
Blue sea slaps against the rocks
Sea rushes around

Clouds high in blue sky
Float smoothly above rivers
Making different shapes

Hailstones bounce around
Sun and rain make a rainbow
After storm has gone.

Rebekah Kay Woodward (9)
Gilberdyke Primary School

Sea - Haikus

Sea sparkling away,
Blue sky starts reflecting down,
People see calm sea.

Sun picks up water,
People start running away,
Cos clouds are dripping.

Rain falls silently,
Sun sparkles making rainbows,
With special colours.

Liquid passing through,
Rivers gleaming in the sun,
Dolphins jumping up.

Whales squirt water out,
Brave fishermen hunt the seas,
For cod and haddock.

Laura Sims (10)
Gilberdyke Primary School

Eleanor

Eyes as blue as the sea.
Face like a peach.
Hair as blonde as spaghetti.
Lips like a red rose.
Top as white as snow.
Cardigan like the blue sky.
Nose as pale as the sand.
Mouth as wide as a whale's.
Eyebrows as brown as a plank of wood.
Teeth as white as milk.
Chin like a bony skeleton.
Canines as pointy as a knife.
Skin like a pink piece of paper.

Eleanor Bielby (8)
Gilberdyke Primary School

The Water Cycle Works - Haikus

Waves go low, leap high.
Splish-splash as a wave goes past.
Crashing hard round rocks.

Fluffy clouds, white-grey,
Moving, swaying, floating by,
Changing shapes all day.

Pitter-patter rain.
Pouring rain falling downwards.
Starting to spit now.

Arched rainbow above.
Shimmers, sparkles, shines so bright.
Pot of gold maybe.

Snowman freezing cold.
Fluffy snow hiding green grass.
Snowflakes flutter down.

Paris Louise Share (10)
Gilberdyke Primary School

James

My face is like a ball.
My face is as round as a pond.
My hair is as short as a rabbit's.
My eyes are as blue as the sea.
My mouth is as small as a fish's.
My ears are as big as a dog's.
My nose is like a dog's.
My teeth are as shiny as a star.

James Whitton (8)
Gilberdyke Primary School

The Water Poem - Haiku

Big sea shimmery
Blue water with shiny fish
Crashing whales leaping

Seawater makes mist
White clouds form and glide in sky
Down it comes, I'm blind

Rain, hail, sleet and snow
Lightning forks hit the ground, *boom!*
Loud thunder goes *crash!*

They start in mountains
Rivers flow into the sea
Start over again

Big sea shimmery
Blue water with shiny fish
Crashing whales leaping.

Tom Collins (10)
Gilberdyke Primary School

Sky

Eyes like a brown crystal.
Nose as small as a tiny teddy bear's.
Mouth as soft as silk.
Eyebrows as brown as a brown horse.
Lips as red as red lipstick.
Teeth like a shark's teeth.
Canines as sharp as a dog's canines.
Tongue as red as a rose.
Chin as hard as a table.
Forehead as white as snow.
Ears as small as a mini egg.

Sky Duke (7)
Gilberdyke Primary School

Blue Sea - Haikus

Blue sea going crash
Massive sharks eating small fish
Salty waves smack rocks

Clouds float in blue skies
Looking like white cotton wool
Some clouds turn thick black

Rain and hail fall down
Rainbows come from rain and sun
Sleet is sloppy snow

Rivers, huge and blue
Flowing fast, dangerously
Leading to the sea

Blue sea going *crash*
Massive sharks eating small fish
Salty waves smack rocks.

Ted Sefton (10)
Gilberdyke Primary School

The Storm - Cinquains

Bang! Bang!
Rumbles the storm
Thunder booms suddenly
Lightning strikes terrifyingly
Silence

Quiet
Birds start to sing
Nature's refreshed again
Rainbows appear in the bright sky
Finished.

Louis Turner (11)
Gilberdyke Primary School

Olivia

Face as round as the moon
Eyes hazel like a hazelnut
Hair as soft as silk
Mouth like a big wide opening
Ears like a round circle
Nose soft like silk
Freckles as small as dots
Eyebrows as brown as a tree trunk
Lips as red as a heart
Teeth as white as clouds
Canines as sharp as a razor
Incisors as strong as a brick
Tongue as red as strawberries
Chin as tough as a tree
Cheeks as soft as wool
Forehead as hard as a fence.

Olivia Maddison (7)
Gilberdyke Primary School

Amelia

Hair as soft as velvet
Eyes as blue as the sea
Face as round as a ball
Nose as thin as a worm
Chin as little as a butterfly
Glasses as clear as crystal
Eyebrows as straight as a ruler
Lips as pink as candyfloss
Teeth as white as a cloud
Canines as sharp as a shark's
Incisors as big as a rock
Tongue as red as a cherry
Cheeks as peachy as sand.

Amelia Marrison (8)
Gilberdyke Primary School

Chelsea

I have a face tipped to the side like a duck.
I have a face as round as a circle.
Brown and blonde hair like leaves.
Hair as curly as a willow tree.
I have eyes as blue as the sea.
I have a mouth, peachy as a flamingo.
I have hidden ears like a mouse in the grass.
I have a nose as wide as a book.
I have eyebrows as brown as a tree trunk.
I have lips as peachy as a colouring pencil.
I have teeth as white as a cloud.

Chelsea Sharman (8)
Gilberdyke Primary School

Elliott

Face like a ball.
Hair like a tiger's skin.
Eyes as brown as muck.
Mouth as chatty as a football match.
Ears as big as an elephant's.
Nose as small as a mouse's.
Eyebrows as brown as a tree trunk.
Lips like pink crystal.
Teeth as sharp as a knife.
Canines as sharp as a shark's.
Incisors as small as pebbles.
Tongue as strong as a strong man's.
Chin as hard as a rock.
Cheeks as red as a rose.
Forehead as big as a whale's.
That's me!

Elliott Stone (7)
Gilberdyke Primary School

Me And Myself

Face as soft as velvet
Hair as black as the night sky
Eyes as brown as a light brown leaf
Mouth as pink as a pink crayon
Ears as light as a shell
Nose as soft as a cushion
Freckles as brown as brown leaves
Eyebrows as furry as a cat's
Lips as red as a red rose
Teeth as white as the moon
Canines as sharp as a shark's teeth
Incisors as small as a mouse's paw
Tongue as rough as sandpaper
Chin as smooth as rubber
Cheeks as rosy as a red pencil sharpener
Forehead as smooth as a sheet.

Chloe Bentley (8)
Gilberdyke Primary School

The Night

The stars are out,
the night is bright,
lights are off, everyone's asleep,
the moon is at its height.

The stars shine up in the sky,
like a diamond in a cave,
the moon gets brighter
like a golden, glowing dish.

The stars are happy
and dancing like fairies,
a shooting star lights up the sky
to guide the animals to their dens.

Connor Luke Dobson (8)
Gilberdyke Primary School

Water Changes - Haikus

Spring:
Mountain water cool,
Rivers filled with slimy fish,
Playing frantically.

Summer:
Out come paddling pools,
Weather is getting warmer,
There has been no rain.

Autumn:
Seas become too rough,
Weather is getting colder,
Puddles appearing.

Winter:
Down come huge raindrops,
Turning into hard hailstones,
Soon it will be spring.

Toby Conboy (10)
Gilberdyke Primary School

Adam

Eyes as big as the sky
Mouth as big as a pencil case
Ears as curly as spaghetti
Nose the size of a lion's
Teeth as strong as metal
Tongue as wriggly as a worm
Hair as blond as a lion's skin.

Adam Salisbury (8)
Gilberdyke Primary School

Seasons In Water - Haikus

Spring:
Drizzles of rain fall
In the mountain starts a spring
Seas covering sand

Summer:
Swimming pools are great
Especially in summer
There's water around

Autumn:
Gentle streams trickle
Drifting leaves in calm water
Drip-drop of light rain

Winter:
Frozen lakes are cool
Foamy seas as cold as ice
Skies as white as snow.

Harry Roy Walker (11)
Gilberdyke Primary School

Rebecca

Eyes the colour of the sky.
Teeth like shiny stars when I smile.
Hair as shiny as the sun.
A mouth as smiley as the sunshine.
Canines as sharp as a vampire's.
Ears as floppy as an elephant's.
Nose like a cat's.
That's me.

Rebecca Routledge (7)
Gilberdyke Primary School

Water Glistening - Haikus

Spring:
Spring water trickles
Through rivers calmly it goes
Fish swim in rivers.

Summer:
River water flows
Shimmering softly, gently
Fish swim around lakes.

Autumn:
Leaves floating in streams
River water is trickling
Glistening clear water.

Winter:
White snow on the ground
Frozen leaves in the water
Ships in stormy seas.

Stephanie Whitton (10)
Gilberdyke Primary School

Andrew

My eyes are as blue as the sea.
My lips are as red as a rose.
My hair is as black as the night.
My teeth are as white as some paper.
My tongue is as pink as a pig's.
My chin is as peachy as a bald cat.
My eyebrows are as brown as a plank of wood.

Andrew Winchester (7)
Gilberdyke Primary School

Water Sparkling

Spring:
Spring lambs
Lapping up the blue water
In the lake beyond.

Summer:
Water is sparkling
Fish swimming in the deep blue
Gold tails flickering

Autumn:
Autumn-coloured leaves
Crunchy, crisp leaves are crunching
Under people's feet

Winter:
Icicles in caves
Shining like a clear diamond
Sleeping bears snoring.

Abigail Ibbotson (9)
Gilberdyke Primary School

Aimee

My hair is as soft as a feather.
My eyebrows are as soft as velvet.
My teeth are as shiny as crystals.
My freckles are as spotty as sand.
My eyes are as blue as a whale's.
My face is as big as a pond.
I have cheeks as red as a rose.
My eyelashes are like sweeping brushes.
My pupils are as black as tadpoles.

Aimee Gregson (7)
Gilberdyke Primary School

Water Forms

Huge waves come
Water trickles from the sky
People having fun.

People swimming in the sea
Everybody's playing
Having fun on the sands

Leaves fallen from trees
Leaves rattling
Leaves bury the land

Snow trickles from skies
Snowmen growing on the snow
Christmas trees stand on the snow.

Daniel David Routledge (10)
Gilberdyke Primary School

Water Seasons

Spring:
Water trickling,
Sun glistening, glimmering,
Rivers calm, so cool.

Summer:
A crest of a wave,
Water flowing gracefully,
A fish racing frantically.

Autumn:
Water trickles down,
Leaves swaying side to side,
Floating in water.

Winter:
Deep, dark depths below,
Blustering oceans roaring,
Rivers all frozen.

Emma Holt (10)
Gilberdyke Primary School

Water In Seasons - Haikus

Spring:
Water is sparkling
Runs down a glistening, clear stream
Gurgle, gurgle, splash

Summer:
Pools filled up, *splash! Splash!*
Children having fun outside
Having water fights

Autumn:
Crunch, crunch, go the leaves
Falling off the fiery trees
Whirling leaves fall down

Winter:
Winter cold and dull
Ice is frozen everywhere
Footprints in the snow.

Keeley Mogg (11)
Gilberdyke Primary School

Water, Water Everywhere - Haikus

Streams trickle down hills,
Water pours into my cup
Water in teapots.

Still waters float past,
Elegant white horses drift,
Streams, rivers, dams, seas.

Seven seas get deep
There's hot water, cold water,
Wind blows leaves on trees.

Icebergs glide past ships,
Frosty ice in rivers flow,
Puddles are frozen.

Daniel Fozard (9)
Gilberdyke Primary School

Water Ways

Spring:
Rain is rushing down
Rain blurred, buds awakening
Charming flowers grow

Summer:
Frogs hop to lilies
Bees hover over flowers
Kids swimming in pools

Autumn:
Eerie trees surround
Myriad leaves float down streams
Wind blows leafy trees.

Winter:
Glaring frosty breeze
Fields covered in soft white snow
As the snowflakes fall.

Bronwen Alice Hall (10)
Gilberdyke Primary School

The Storm Crashing - Cinquains

Crashing
Bright, striking light.
Shaking from head to toe.
Hiding under soft warm covers.
Shocking.

Happy.
Lights back on now.
Cuddle from Mum and Dad.
Kettle boiling for drink tonight.
Quiet.

Christopher Jackson (11)
Gilberdyke Primary School

Water Changes - Haikus

Spring:
Blossom in rivers
Floating swiftly down in streams
Hedgehogs drink from bowls.

Summer:
Calm waves are quiet
Deep rivers flowing gently
Bears hunting for fish.

Autumn:
Waves getting choppy
Ripple, crashing against cliffs
It starts to hailstone

Winter:
Water turns to ice
Icy ponds waiting for skates
High hopes spring will come!

Amy Norton (10)
Gilberdyke Primary School

Funfair

The funfair is a good place to be,
lots of rides for you to see.
Find the ride you like the best,
on you pop till you can't stop.

Go in the night, you will see the lights,
colours like jewels, sparkling so bright.

Noises all around of children having fun,
twirling, whirling round and round,
like a whirlwind on the ground.

Bethany Share (9)
Gilberdyke Primary School

Water Dribbling - Haikus

Spring:
Water dribbling down
Cold rain trickles down my nose
Shining everywhere.

Summer:
There's no rain in sight
All you need is some water
Everybody sweats.

Autumn:
Myriad leaves fall
Rapidly floating downwards
Rain falls down on trees.

Winter:
Icicles hang down
Everybody likes the snow
Snow is freezing cold.

Kelly Huby (10)
Gilberdyke Primary School

Fantastic Fish

Fish swim everywhere in the world,
They all live in the sea, curled.
Some are big, some are small,
Some are short, some are tall.

People think they're all vicious,
But when they're cooked they're delicious.
There are all kinds of fishes,
Like sharks and lots more dishes.

Daniel Shaw (9)
Gilberdyke Primary School

Water All Around - Haikus

Spring:
As blue as the sky
Water starts to get warmer
Fishing for great pikes

Summer:
People on a cruise
More people come to the beach
Water is so cool

Autumn:
Leaves whirl down from trees
Lots of leaves in the river
It rains more often

Winter:
Water gets frozen
Frost is spread around gardens
Water gets too cold.

Scott Davy (11)
Gilberdyke Primary School

In The Night

In the night things come out,
creepy monsters, wolves and foxes,
they come to eat you in the night.

In the night monsters as big as hills,
wolves as strong as elephants
and foxes as fast as cheetahs,
come to eat you in the night!

Joe Sefton (9)
Gilberdyke Primary School

Water In Seasons - Haikus

Spring:
Lilies flowering
Glistening in calm water
Fish darting below

Summer:
The sparkling water
Busy beaches everywhere
Kids splashing in pool

Autumn:
Turning rough, stormy
Eerie mist surrounding you
Getting icier

Winter:
Violent water
Waves as giant as mountains
Ice is all around.

Ben Lister (10)
Gilberdyke Primary School

Water Frozen Solid - Haikus

Spring:
Oceans dance quiet
Sea creatures come out to play
In the ocean's light

Summer:
Rivers are joyful:
They are happy as the day
Magnificent streams

Autumn:
The sea fogs roll in
Algae floats on the water
Oceans become rough

Winter:
Everything is still
All water's frozen solid
Icicles dangle.

Devon Thompson (9)
Gilberdyke Primary School

Water In The Seasons

Spring:
Spring's sparkling seas
On a calm day waves are smooth
Water-hopping lizards.

Summer:
Blossom in water.
Fine weather for boats at sea
Waves on the sea.

Autumn:
Crispy leaves on water.
Dead of activity, silent.
Rough seas thrashing boats.

Winter:
Unbelievably cold.
Life-threatening, fishermen.
Brilliant ice-skating.

James Barnes (11)
Gilberdyke Primary School

Water - Haikus

Spring
Rivers calm in spring
Streams are flowing smoothly down
All nicely calm, soft.

Summer:
Waves are moving quick
Extremely carefully now
Crashing all around.

Autumn:
Seas getting rougher
Blue whales are roaring loudly
Swaying through darkness.

Winter:
Beautifully smooth
Ice shining with a sparkle
Children skating fast.

Benjamin Kitching (10)
Gilberdyke Primary School

A Year With Nature

In summer the sky is blue like a blue carpet.
The grass is emerald-green and the roses are ruby-red.
The hedgehogs hunt for slugs and worms for lunch
And the birds sing like choir people.
The rabbits hop like frogs and eat grass and carrots.
The trees are covered with leaves and apples
And the birds nest there too.

In spring, the flowers begin to grow even bigger than before
And the trees have blossom so hummingbirds come to drink.
Baby chicks are born and baby lambs are born too.

Autumn is when the leaves on the trees turn brown, orange and red,
The flowers go brown and solid and the birds fly south.

In winter it snows like pieces of cotton wool falling from the sky
And people build snowmen and snowballs.
Robins come out to play and Santa brings presents.

Beth Dredge (9)
Gilberdyke Primary School

Easter Eggs

I like Easter eggs, they're yummy and scrummy.
I like to feel the chocolate melting on my tongue.

They have colourful and shiny wrappers and they're very, very tasty.
They shine like a bright planet up in the sky.

They come in many sizes from small to large.
They hold many secrets deep inside.

I love to eat Easter eggs although they make you fat,
But the centres are so dreamy, I don't really care about that.

Shannon Lucy Rastrick (8)
Gilberdyke Primary School

Seals

I love seals when they flip and flap,
Splashing in the water like a swimmer,
They are excellent at diving,
Catching food for their supper,
Seals are shiny when they come out of the water.

Shiny coats that glow like glitter,
Flapping their powerful flipper,
Seals eat fish and plankton,
Dolphins are a seal's best friend,
They slip onto the shore and eat a fishy dish
And share it with their family.

They make a sound like a dog barking when they play around,
But while they're hunting, they don't make a sound,
They can balance balls on their noses for children to watch,
They flap their flippers together.
Oh I think seals are clever.

Katie Louise Last (8)
Gilberdyke Primary School

The Dog

My dog runs like a shooting star.
When he has a bath he looks like a rat, all skinny.
He loves to roll in the bright sunshine.

He sniffs at everything from flowers to food.
He has a toilet stop at every corner.
He makes friends with other dogs and barks like a wolf.

He sleeps in a cage on a big, softy, cuddly pillow.
He settles in a big ball in front of a warm fire.
I love my cute dog.

Megan Malcolmson (9)
Gilberdyke Primary School

A Furry Dog

A furry dog is as fluffy as a cloud
And loves pouncing around
And when she whines she makes me cry
But sometimes she makes me smile.

My dog is as happy as a birthday
When I give her a hug
And never barks out loud
When she rolls on the rug.

My dog loves treats
Like juicy, big bones
She will never bite or scratch me
She likes to have a play.

My dog loves me, I know she does
She can't tell me
But together we're a pair.

Lauren Champion (9)
Gilberdyke Primary School

Leopards

A leopard is as creepy as a ghost,
They hide in green grass,
They hunt their tasty prey,
They jump as high as a butterfly,
They touch the beautiful sky
And chase them away.

Jack Copley (8)
Gilberdyke Primary School

The Cat In The Hat

The cat in the hat,
sits on a mat,
trying to catch a rat,
what do you think of that?

The cat in the hat,
holding a bat,
eating the mat,
what do you think of that?

The cat in the hat,
asleep on the mat,
getting quite fat,
what do you think of that?

The cat in the hat
as quiet as a rat,
now what do you think of that?

Amanda Winchester (9)
Gilberdyke Primary School

The Star In The Night

The wind was a deluge of darkness,
Among the blustering trees.
The moon was a spectral galleon,
Tossed upon overcast seas.
The sky was a magnitude of twilight,
Above the lilac moors,
And there in the distance
A sparkling star shone,
            shimmering,
                    glistening,
Over a magnificent palace's marble walls.

Ryan Thorne (10)
Hornsea Community Primary School

Outside The Classroom Window I Saw . . .

Outside the classroom window I saw
Trees twiddle their thumbs and wait patiently,
The fence guard the school against intruders,
The grass dance and prance in the howl of the wind,
The playground support children as they played,
The clouds sail a long voyage across the deep blue sky,
The sun poke its way through the deep darkness of the night,
The street light stand and flash, conducting a symphony of traffic,
And the cars battle through a forest of metal.

Tyler Fletcher (10)
Hornsea Community Primary School

My Washing Machine

My washing machine's huge,
My washing machine's small,
My washing machine's marvellous,
My washing machine's tall,
My washing machine's got a monster inside it.

A monster inside it?
Yep.

It growls and it creaks,
It whispers and it peeps,
It doesn't think we know it's there,

But I know,

I've seen it about,
Stealing crisps and juice from downstairs.

My washing machine's got a monster inside it.
A monster inside it?
Yep.

Maddie Walton (10)
Hornsea Community Primary School

Outside The Classroom Window . . .

Outside the classroom window . . .
The trees twiddled their thumbs and waited patiently,
The fence groaned and moaned as the wind blew,
The grass stood like a blade of iron as the gentle breeze went by,
The playground shivered as it turned into an ice cube,
The clouds gently navigated the crystal-blue sky,
The streetlights flickered and flashed as night drew in,
The cars barged their way through the tarmac and concrete.

Megan Gell (10)
Hornsea Community Primary School

The Football Match

The crowd was cheering that cold afternoon,
Twenty-two men stood still.
The whistle blew loud,
The ball sailed high,
Liverpool and Everton in a battle of will.

Ten minutes of passing from striker to midfield,
Keeper, defender and back.
A shot at the goal, hit the crossbar, and in
Liverpool was now on the track.

The score at half-time was one-all,
Everton headed it hard in the net.
The pitch was a mud bath,
The referee was blind,
Liverpool had more goals to get.

One minute to go, a penalty shot,
Gerrard was just getting up.
He was panting and nervous,
But he kicked straight and true,
And of course Liverpool won the Cup!

George Anthony (11)
Hornsea Community Primary School

Where Dead Bodies Lie . . .

Down in the basement where frightful ghosts lurk,
Something lies dead, dead in the dirt,
And not knowing what to do,
I need to escape, I want to!

Cobwebs and beetles crawling over me,
The dust is unbearable, it's too wet to see,
The floor is wet,
But I am set
For anything nasty and dangerous.

A spooky noise, probably the wind,
Oh my goodness, I feel I'm going to cringe.
The fire torches burning
In my stomach which is churning.

Howling werewolves in the moonlight,
This is not my usual Friday night,
This is like a death fright
I need to escape - right!

Olivia Clubley (10)
Hornsea Community Primary School

My Cat

Tabitha, that's the name of my cat.
She is white and brown and rather too fat,
She runs and plays and chases mice all day.
She loves me and adores to play,
She always appears when food is around,
And an empty bowl is always found.
She is one out of four,
And I certainly don't want any more.

Adam Bodsworth (10)
Hornsea Community Primary School

The Portal

Through the magic window I saw
A vortex demolishing everything in its path.

Through the magic window I saw
Money descending from the indigo sky.

Through the magic window I saw
A blood-red lake overflow onto the banks of toffee.

Through the magic window I saw
Divers swimming through the Fanta sea,
Trying to discover the marshmallow fish.

Through the magic window I saw
Cars racing on the green tarmac, crashing into the candy trees.

Through the magic window I saw
A milk chocolate waterfall descending like a person
Falling from a liquorice plane.

Through the magic window I saw
A bundle of planes with engines as loud as a football crowd.

Through the magic window I saw
Sharks lurking beneath the murky waters.

Josh Cooper (10)
Hornsea Community Primary School

Hippo Hiccups!

My hippo has the hiccups,
And his hiccups shake the ground!
The floor is always rumbling,
When my hippo is around!

Lucy Bell (11)
Hornsea Community Primary School

The Sea

The sea is like a million sapphires crammed together
on a soft and cosy liquid-crystal blanket.
The sea is like trees swaying calmly and gently through
the breeze on a warm summer's morning.
The sea crashes and bashes against the cliffs,
like an army charging into battle, when it seems like all is lost
and there is nothing else to lose.
The sea is like a black hole engulfing you into a black doom,
with no hope of finding a way out.
The sea is like a hammer crushing everything in its path,
nothing can stop it.
The sea is like a beautiful goddess of serenity.

Joseph Whincup (11)
Hornsea Community Primary School

Dragon!

Fog swirled around its bulging feet,
Two sharpened toes stuck out.
Its scaly legs looked like thousands of sharp blades.
Knobbly knees joined its hips and shins,
Its hips were circular, just as scaly as its legs.

Its stomach bellowed out below its waist,
Scaly arms were joined to its spiky fingers.
Nails looked like gigantic spikes,
Menacing elbows connected powerful biceps to triceps.

Teeth shot like devastating daggers.
Fire shot from its mouth, colliding with the rock face
The dragon stood proud and strong.
Master of the mountains.

Adam Railton (11)
Hornsea Community Primary School

I Looked Out Of The Window Last night

I looked out of the window last night . . .
I saw scintillating stars glistening,
In the jet-black night.

I looked out of the window last night . . .
I saw the immense crescent moon,
Lying on its back; high in the sky.

I looked out of the window last night . . .
I saw the city in the dead of night,
Silhouetted for all its worth.

I closed the curtains last night . . .
Leaving behind,
The magic of the black,
                black,
                    black,
                        night.

Dan Wilkinson (10)
Hornsea Community Primary School

Waterfall

W ashing over the ragged, murky rocks,
A ccelerating over the edge like a cheetah.
T ipping itself closer and closer into the foaming pool below,
E legantly escaping the calmness of the river.
R oaring as it hits the frothy waters beneath.
F rothy fragments fly off the amazing column,
A rching high over the rock face.
L urching into the gloomy darkness,
L eading to more tranquil waters.

Waterfall - nature's beautiful beast!

Thomas Catley (11)
Hornsea Community Primary School

Daisy!

The whispering of the rolling waves
Was accompanied by the gentle crunching of sand underfoot,
As we strolled along the sun-kissed beach,
Lost in peaceful thoughts floating in our minds,
Happy in the belief that the tranquillity would last forever,
How wrong we could be!
Ambling along in peaceful harmony,
Without a care in the world,
When suddenly our dreams were shattered by a distant yelping.
Slowly, we could hear the thrashing and splashing of stones,
                                        sand and water
As a ball of legs and tails and fur came hurtling towards us.
Thrashing up sand in all directions,
She came at great speed,
Causing mayhem and madness,
But bringing a pleasure all of her own.
Not peace and quiet but wild happiness -
Dizzy, daft, deafening, drooling, dancing,
Delightful Daisy.
Her moments of madness brought squeals of delight from us all.
The peace would return later, but for now
Our dog will drive us crazy.
                    Crazy Daisy!

Ellie Senior-Farmer (10)
Hornsea Community Primary School

Lonely Night

A place by the fire in my old armchair,
I am alone with no one my fire to share.
The crackling of logs burning bright,
Consoling in my weary plight.

Shadows playing on the ceiling and wall,
Ghosts past and present coming to call.
Outside, the wind howls and moans,
Reminding me of my aching bones.

I am in the grip of a hole too deep,
Just past my garden I could not keep.
A fleeting glimpse of happiness long past,
With the echoes of words spoken too fast.

A candle in the window to light the way,
To any lost soul that wants to stay.
All are welcome to a place by my fire,
This is my wish, my one desire.

Loneliness is what I fear the most,
I am willing to play the welcoming host.
Come along, guided by my candle's light,
And help me pass this lonely night.

Kieran Baines (10)
Hornsea Community Primary School

White

White is . . .

Frosty snowflakes silhouetting the baby-blue sky,
A flock of delicate doves scattering the horizon,
Frothy whipped cream hugging rosy-red strawberries,
An elegant swan gliding across a turquoise lagoon,
A wild rabbit hopping gracefully amongst a colourful flower bed,
Luxury marshmallows bathing in creamy chocolate,
Pure clean washing hanging on a taut washing line,
A minute mouse squeaking like a dog's chewy toy.

White is supreme.

Sadie Dickson (11)
Hornsea Community Primary School

The Sea

The sea is . . .
White horses riding across a blue carpet

The sea is . . .
A turquoise-aquamarine land far beyond the horizon

The sea is . . .
A blue robe hugging the shore, an influence to all

The sea is . . .
A whistling wild howl in the midnight sky

The sea is . . .
Swimming in a large pool of freezing cold saltwater

The sea is . . .
A home to many and all around,
It's a living to others, it's sight and sound

The sea is . . .
Unpredictable . . . it's ever-changing . . . unique!
Just like me!

Laura Smith (11)
Hornsea Community Primary School

My Window

Outside my window
I saw the fence standing like a centurion waiting for battle.

Outside my window
I saw the grass dancing like a ballet dancer in a show.

Outside my window
I saw the roundabout spinning like an Olympic discus thrower.

Outside my window
I saw the stones being thrown like bullets in the discouraged gale.

Outside my window
I saw clouds like graceful galleons gliding across the sky.

Inside my window
Is the place to be.

Liam Moffat (10)
Hornsea Community Primary School

Homework

Some people hate homework.
Some people like homework.

Some people think homework
Is a waste of time.
Some people think homework
Kills time.

Some people think homework
Is boring.
Some people think homework
Is fun.

But I *hate* homework!

Josh Beck (11)
Hornsea Community Primary School

Autumn

The summer's sun has faded, the frosty breeze creeps near.
The crisp leaves fade and turn to murky brown.
Squirrels scurry silently to seek something special.
Many months they've waited to claim what now is theirs.
Conkers cautiously launch down to the Earth's surface clasped by
the autumn air.
As the summer perishes, the bleak of autumn arrives.
The luxury of having crisp, cool air and conker fights will soon
be here to share.

Jasmin Dearing (10)
Hornsea Community Primary School

In My Mind

In my mind I saw . . .
A cascading waterfall,
Shimmering in the daytime sun,
Like strings of pearl necklaces.

In my mind I saw . . .
Energetic monkeys swinging from tree to tree,
In the heart of the lonely jungle.

In my mind I heard . . .
The sound of a slithering snake,
Searching for its prey.

In my mind I saw . . .
An elegant eagle soaring through the midnight sky,
Like a plane getting ready to land,
Looking for its feathered friends.

In my mind I heard . . .
The song of a humpback whale,
Like a haunted spirit,
Lonely forever.

Brooke Knight (11)
Hornsea Community Primary School

Trains

The train in the station, long and lonely,
Waiting for its next journey.
The train hissing and warm,
Now taking passengers out of the cold.
It sets off puffing and steaming,
Leaving the station,
Silver rails gleaming,
Faster and faster into the night.
Slicing through the darkness, towards the edge of dawn,
Hundreds of miles away,
The grey light of morning,
No hero's welcome for two men that have delivered
Two hundred people into the various paths of their lives,
To begin another day.

Matthew Sinar (10)
Hornsea Community Primary School

Water

The water ripples through the streams,
Flows through the long, deep rivers,
Sits quietly on the enormous lakes
While the delicate swans swim gracefully.
The pond water teems with tiny fish,
Hiding amongst the long swaying reeds.
In the harbour the water is gentle,
A small wave rocks the bright orange dinghies to and fro.
Waves gently lap against the shore,
Like stroking a newborn puppy.
Whales and dolphins pop up out of nowhere,
Mermaids play with snapping crabs,
Joyful fish swirl and dance under the sea.

Katy Brooks (11)
Hornsea Community Primary School

A Rose

A rose is a butterfly's cave where he lurks,
secretly sucking the life out of the beautiful flower.

It can be charming or a weapon of mass destruction,
piercing through the skin of an unfortunate victim.

It is a sculpture of essence, giving vibrance to the room
where it is displayed.

A crimson sun, setting beyond the darkness
of the gloomy horizon.

It is an umbrella of ruby, cloaking the emerald, skinny stalk
from danger.

A rose is the Earth's perfume, giving magnificent aroma,
joy and happiness to all the things that smell it.

Liam Tudor-Bateman (11)
Hornsea Community Primary School

Joy

Joy, what a joy,
What a life without a name,
Proud to be what it is.

Sad, what a cry,
What a life without a name,
Hard to show what it is.

Crime, what a crime,
What a life without a name,
Showing around the world.

Joy, what a joy,
Sad, what a cry,
Crime, what a crime,
Without a name,
Proud to be what it is!

Jessica Beevers (11)
Hornsea Community Primary School

The World Turned Upside Down Today!

The world turned upside down today, please don't ask me why,
My dad was using the litter box, whilst my cat was wearing a tie.
My brother was taking Mum for a walk in the park.
My dog was making us toast,
My 80-year-old grandma was confidently windsurfing
Down on the coast.
The gerbil was playing with Barbie dolls
As my sister spun on a wheel,
My auntie was swimming around in a tank
Whilst the fish were wearing high heels.
Grandpa was sucking a dummy
Whilst the baby smoked a cigar!
All I could scream, all I could shout was,
'Help, the world's gone bizarre!'

Holly Brown (11)
Hornsea Community Primary School

Autumn Fires

In the other gardens
And all up the vale,
From the autumn bonfires
See the smoke trail!

Mellow summer finished
And all the summer flowers,
The red fire blazes
The grey smoke towers.

Chant or hum a song of seasons
Something clear in all,
Flowers blooming in the summer
Fires flame in the fall!

Amy Jenney (11)
Hornsea Community Primary School

Chocolate

Who can't resist this sticky brown delight?
Melting in my mouth,
Swirling in my mouth
Brown fluffy clouds like Heaven in my mouth.

It's hard in the freezer,
Soft near the fire.
It's addictive and naughty,
It's your lifelong desire.

There are so many varieties,
So much to choose.
Scrumptious strawberry,
Creamy and cool.

A countless selection,
Of this lovely sweet.
Mars bars and Snickers.
Oooh! Such a treat.

My
   My
      Oh
         My

It's sooo good to eat!

Amber Softley (11)
Hornsea Community Primary School

Growing Up

I opened my eyes,
What did I see?
A scary doctor's face
Looking down at me.

I rode my first bike,
It had only three wheels,
I took it everywhere,
I sat on it when I had meals.

When I was three, I started nursery,
It was my first experience with school,
I can remember
That it was great and that I felt very cool.

I started primary school
And made various friends,
I played countless games
And learned about latest trends.

I came to the end
Of my primary school life,
I am growing up, I thought,

What a fab life!

Emily Williams (11)
Hornsea Community Primary School

The Horse

Eyes - alert, sparkling, ever watching for danger.
Ears - pointing, listening for danger.
Mane - thick and flowing in the wind.
Tail - swishing, swatting flies.
Hoove - of thunder, strong and tough.
Muzzle - soft as velvet on the palm of my hand.
Shoulders - powerful, round, rippling muscle.
Back - solid and strong to carry me home.

The horse - a kind and gentle creature.
My loyal, trusting friend

Tessa Watson (10)
Hornsea Community Primary School

Clouds

Clouds are like
Thick, fluffy cotton wool balls
Flying in mid-air
Bobbing rabbits' tails
Waggling in the emerald forest

Bouncy candyfloss
Scrambling around the dark velvet sky
An immaculate thrown-out duvet
Which lies in the dirty dustbin

Like thrown-up pieces of paper
Jumped into the cerulean sky.
Clouds are flawless.

Jack Shepherd (11)
Hornsea Community Primary School

Outside The Classroom Window

Outside the classroom window I saw . . .
The trees swaying side to side waiting patiently.

Outside the classroom window I saw . . .
The fence shiver in the cold air.

Outside the classroom window I saw . . .
The grass sharply fight its way through the other grass.

Outside the classroom window I saw . . .
The lonely playground waiting for someone to talk to.

Outside the classroom window I saw . . .
The clouds floating in the clear blue sky.

Outside the classroom window I saw . . .
The sun fighting his way out of the darkness from the night.

Outside the classroom window I saw . . .
The cars scarper their way through the dark forests.

Outside the classroom window I saw . . .
The street lights flicker in the cold, sooty air.

Libby Wallwork (10)
Hornsea Community Primary School

Water Is . . .

A cerulean sheet overlapping the world,
A cobalt sea pushing away the golden sand.
An ultramarine ocean tearing land piece by painful piece,
A planet, the colour of Pluto.
The liquid we live on,
A super-sensory ray filling up any space.
A dangerous place for land-living creatures,
An extremely fast being that soaks all in its path.
A luminous liquid that glitters in the sunlight,
An essential for life, essential to all of *us!*

James Oliphant (10)
Hornsea Community Primary School

Chocolate For Life

Through the magic window I saw
a marshmallow mountain embedded with green jelly sweets
overlooking a gingerbread town.

Through the magic window I saw
a chocolate river flowing lively through a chewing gum estuary.

Through the magic window I saw
a jelly baby gliding across a lake of white whipped cream.

Through the magic window I saw
a waterfall cascading off large pieces of malt toffee.

Through the magic window I saw
a sweet tree littering the ground with chocolate.

Through the magic window I saw
a fountain spitting chocolate chunks all over the floor.

Through the magic window I saw
a jellybaby rowing boiled sweets across a black ocean of
dark chocolate.

Through the magic window I saw
a liquorice swan waddling across a field of green chocolate.

Ben McGill (10)
Hornsea Community Primary School

Dirty Dog

The dirty dog dawdled like a cheeky child
The dirty dog dug down, disturbing the dancing daffodils
The dirty dog sniffed every luminous lamp post along his way
The dirty dog scratched his scruffy fur in the midday sun
The dirty dog grinned at the rigid, rocky, delicious bone

The dirty dog had fabulous fun!

Deanna Postill (10)
Hornsea Community Primary School

Outside The Classroom Window . . .

The trees twiddle their thumbs and wait patiently.
The fence persuades the unwanted guests to leave
and stays to keep watch.

The grass celebrates and dances with the plants,
adoring the breeze of the air.

The playground allows children to run and play on itself
making all children happy and joyful.

The clouds move about the sky collecting the water
vapour and then slowly make the rain precipitate from the sky.

The sun shines on the people lovingly, wanting the
Earth to never be dark.

The streetlights love the black sheet of darkness
as it is their job to brighten up the night, showing everybody
they should no more be afraid of the dark.

The cars storm through a humongous, everlasting fleet of traffic,
and all the vehicles fight a way through the army.

Daniel Ellmer (11)
Hornsea Community Primary School

The Classroom Window

Outside my classroom window,
Trees gossip and gurgle all day long.

The fence sways and wobbles in the gusting wind
And grass dances and sings in the whistling wind.

The playground is shrieking with fear of the children's footsteps
As they run about and play.

The clouds finish painting themselves the colours of the rainbow.

Ashleigh Metcalf (10)
Hornsea Community Primary School

Room 13

I went to the crow's nest,
It was the trip I liked the best.

What did I see?
Well, well, well

Well I saw,
The bed of dread.

What else did I see?
Well, well, well

Well I saw,
The room of gloom
And the bed of dread.

What else did I see?
Well, well, well

Well I saw,
A rat with a hat
And the room of gloom
And the bed of dread.

What else did I see?
Well, well, well

Well I saw,
A skeleton without a head dancing on the bed
And a rat with a hat
And the room of gloom
And the bed of dread.

What else did I see?
Well, well, well

Well I saw
A skeleton without a head dancing on the bed
And a puddle of blood that was red
And a rat with a hat
And a bat
And the room of gloom
With a tomb
And the bed of dread
And someone who was dead.

Charlie Kelly (10)
Hornsea Community Primary School

Through The Portal

This is where the journey begins,
we will witness the treasures beyond.
As the feeling grows it will start to end . . .
but first we need a beginning.

Through the magic portal it goes,
a quite distracting line,
as this starts I will think and hope,
so here goes . . .

Through the magic portal I saw a great golden fortress
gliding on an elegant emerald cloud.

Through the magic portal I saw a splendid swan
gliding across the bright blue lake.

Through the magic portal I saw toffee chunks
with a path of chocolate chips that were twirling
and twisting high into the clouds.

Through the magic portal I saw a lamp post
conducting a symphony of traffic, straight along the tarmac.

James Osborne (10)
Hornsea Community Primary School

The Room 13 Poem

We went to the crow's nest
Thought it was the best.

What did I see?
Ask me,
Ask me,
Ask me.

Elle-May did not look her best
She is no more a pest.

What did I see?
Ask me,
Ask me,
Ask me.

I was scared
When I was dared.
Elle-May did not look her best
She is no more a pest.

What else did I see?
Ask me,
Ask me,
Ask me.

I saw a door
When I was on the floor
I was scared
When I was dared
Elle-May did not look her best
She is no more a pest.

Chloe Fitzgerald (11)
Hornsea Community Primary School

Thunder And Lightning

Electric sparking out of a plug,
Gold, alive.
Tridents hailing out of the sky,
Burning, death.
Shattered glass pelting the heavens,
Mass destruction,
The Devil's horns,
Hell, fear.
A shard of silver,
A slash of mercury,
Flickering snakes' tongues.
War of the worlds,
Lightning.

Rifles firing,
Drums beating,
People shouting,
Stomach churning.
Kids thumping,
Windowpanes rattling,
Pans clattering,
A hockey ball smashing the backboard.
Crowds roaring,
Cymbals clashing,
Titans sparring,
Thunder.

Tom Duckworth (11)
Hornsea Community Primary School

The Haunted Poem Of Room 13

In the crow's nest I stormed into the room, it was full of gloom.
What else did I see? Ask me, ask me, ask me!
Well, I saw a skeleton with no head bouncing on the bed.

What else did I see? Ask me, ask me, ask me!
Well, I saw the kite of fright in the middle of the night,
And a skeleton with no head bouncing on the bed.

What else did I see? Ask me, ask me, ask me!
I saw my friend Fred with no eyes, covered in flies,
And I saw the kite of fright in the middle of the night,
And I saw a skeleton with no head bouncing on the bed.
What else did I see? Ask me, ask me, ask me!

Well, I saw a rat with a hat on the mat,
And I saw my friend Fred with no eyes, covered in flies,
And I saw the kite of fright in the middle of the night,
And I saw a skeleton with no head bouncing on the bed
And that's all I saw in room 13.

Adam Yorke (11)
Hornsea Community Primary School

The World

The fence . . . tries to avoid being chopped down.
The grass . . . trembles and shivers in the cold air.
The playground . . . rumbles and screams in the street.
The clouds . . . huff and puff the sun away from the sky.
The sun . . . unbolts itself from the illuminated sky.
The streetlight . . . opens its light for others to see.
The cars . . . speed, desperate to win the trophy.

Lewis Wood (11)
Hornsea Community Primary School

Room 13

I went to the room of doom
and to my fright Dracula was in the room.
What did I see?
I saw a skeleton's head jumping on the bed.

Tell me more.

I saw Lisa on the floor getting chopped up by a chainsaw
and a skeleton's head jumping on the bed.

Tell me more.

I saw a dragon's head on the bed of dread
and Lisa on the floor getting chopped up by a chainsaw
and a skeleton's head jumping on the bed.

Tell me more.

I saw Lisa on the bed with a bullet in her head
and a dragon's head on the bed of dread
and Lisa on the floor getting chopped up by a chainsaw
and a skeleton's head jumping on the bed,

And that's all I saw in the room of doom.

Jay Vaughan (11)
Hornsea Community Primary School

Room Of Doom

I went into the room of doom and then I saw the moon.

What else did I see?

I saw a very big spider spinning a web,
I saw a person dead on the bed.

What else did I see?

The key of death and someone's last breath.
And that's all I saw in the room of doom.

Peter Simms (10)
Hornsea Community Primary School

My Thoughts

Through the magic window I can see,
a chocolate fountain flowing over the shiny strawberries.

Through the magic window I can see,
a giant swimming pool shining in the sunlight.

Through the magic window I can see,
chocolate dolphins jumping over the sparkling waves.

Through the magic window I can see,
blue budgies twittering in the light through a clear blue sky.

Through the magic window I can see,
a steaming hot Margarita pizza and a drink of iced Coke.

Through the magic window I can see,
millions of hot dogs flowing gently across the gleaming blue sky.

Through the magic window I can see,
chocolate foam rushing in from the sea.

Through the magic window I can see,
giant waves crashing in on the gold sandy beach.

Jacob Richards (10)
Hornsea Community Primary School

Through The Magic Window I Saw . . .

Through the magic window I saw
A perfect pink palace perched on a whipped hillside.

Through the magic window I saw
A chocolate river cut through a marshmallow mountain.

Through the magic window I saw
Clouds sail across the crystalline sky.

Through the magic window I saw
A wonderful unicorn with a diamond horn.

Through the magic window I saw
A rainbow leap over a cloudless sky.

Charlie Stork (10)
Hornsea Community Primary School

Through The Window

Through the magic window I saw
a lush grassy meadow with a timbered carriage riding down
the gravelly road.

Through the magic window I saw
a huge chocolate waterfall plummeting down into the fudge rocks.

Through the magic window I saw
an overcast green train carting a herd of cows still in a field.

Through the magic window I saw
a nectar-yellow baboon with a bulky bronze bottom.

Through the magic window I heard
a brass band playing in a graceful hall, with laughter bursting
out from behind the oak doors.

Through the magic window I felt
a luxurious bed of feathers, waiting to be dived into.

Through the magic window I saw
an elegant cream lake with a silky swan flying past.

Amy Sinar (10)
Hornsea Community Primary School

I'm A Fast Racing Car

My name is Kamar, I'm a fast racing car.
I was made in Brazil, living here is a chill,
Flaming red is my colour with a gold shining bumper,
I drink rocket fuel because it makes me look cool.
I start the race and leave the rest in disgrace,
When you hear my sound I rumble to the ground.
As I come to the end I wind the 'S' bend,
To win the race I have to go at a fast pace.
I'm doing one hundred and ten,
Through the chequered flag and the winner's pen!

Ben Samuel (11)
Hornsea Community Primary School

Through My Scene Of Life

Through the classroom window I saw . . .

The grass serenading smoothly a Mexican wave to the world.

The playground waiting for a long-lost friend to appear beside it.

The clouds selling candyfloss and treats to the people of the land.

The sun making its way through the bleak midnight darkness.

The streetlights flickering and conducting a slow symphony
of traffic.

The cars barging, begging, fighting their way through the
colour-cascaded crowd.

The people searching, continuing to hope for their long-lost lovers.

Craig Monkman (10)
Hornsea Community Primary School

Through The Magic Window

Through the magic window,
I felt the smooth syrup slip through my fingers.

Through the magic window,
I stepped in the mud which felt like chocolate melting on my feet.

Through the magic window,
I saw a boat like a banana split.

Through the magic window,
I saw a wonderful unusual unicorn dancing across
the marshmallow mountains.

Through the magic window,
I saw a sugar tree scattering colourful candy to the children.

Abigail Abey (11)
Hornsea Community Primary School

Room 13 Poem

It was gloomy in the room,
And there was a reflection of the moon.
What else did I see?
Ask me, ask me.

I saw a skeleton with no head dancing on the bed.
What else did I see?
Ask me, ask me.

I saw a fright on my right,
A skeleton with no head dancing on the bed.
What else did I see?
Ask me, ask me.

I saw a fright on my right,
And a skeleton with no head dancing on the bed,
I saw the bed of dread.
What else did I see?
Ask me, ask me.

Viki Henderson (11)
Hornsea Community Primary School

Room 13

In the crow's nest there was danger all about,
I heard Dracula shout.
What did I see?

I saw a skeleton dancing on the bed,
I saw a person dead.
What did I see?
Tell me, tell me, tell me.

I saw room 13, I was so keen,
I saw Lisa eating some beans,
I saw a skeleton dancing on the bed,
I saw a person dead.

That's all I saw in the crow's nest!

Jordan Hillerby (11)
Hornsea Community Primary School

My Dreams

Through the magic window I saw
a chocolate fountain splashing over the marshmallow rocks.

Through the magic window I saw
flowers dancing on the pink soda lake.

Through the magic window I saw
a swimming pool made of caramel.

Through the magic window I saw
a super-giant banana split covered from top to toe
with hundreds and thousands.

Through the magic window I saw
pizzas whizzing around trying to find people to eat them.

Through the magic window I saw
caramel penguins dancing away to welcome people.

Through the magic window I saw
a house made out of money.

Through the magic window I saw
people walking around wearing marshmallow slippers.

Danielle Sullivan (11)
Hornsea Community Primary School

Room 13

I saw a locked room,
I looked through, I saw my doom,
What did I see?
What, what, what?

Well,
I saw a pool of blood and a lump of mud.
What else did you see?
What, what, what?

Well,
I saw a head poking out of a piece of lead,
And a pool of blood and a lump of mud.
What else did you see?
What, what, what?

Well,
I saw a skeleton's head on the bed,
And a head poking out of a piece of lead,
And a pool of blood and a lump of mud,
That's what I saw!

Hannah Marsh (10)
Hornsea Community Primary School

Room 13 Poem

I went to room 13.
It was so mean.
What did I see?
Think!
Think!
Think!

Well,
There was a fright
On my right.
What else did I see?
Think!
Think!
Think!

Well,
I saw a jack-in-the-box
Talking to a fox.
And there was a fright
On my right.
What else did I see?
Think!
Think!
Think!

That's all I saw in room 13!

Danielle Gray (10)
Hornsea Community Primary School

Room 13 Poem

I went into the room,
I was filled with gloom.

What did you see?
Please! Tell me.

Well,
I saw a skeleton with no head dancing on the bed.

What else did you see?
Tell me,
Tell me,
Tell me.

Well,
I saw a cat in a hat,
And I saw a skeleton on the bed with no head.

What else did you see?
Tell me,
Tell me,
Tell me.

Well,
I saw Lisa on the bed,
With dread,
And a skeleton on the bed with no head.
That's all I saw.

Dominic Edwards (10)
Hornsea Community Primary School

My Room 13 Poem

I went to the room of doom.
I was filled with lots of gloom,
And what did I see?
Ask me,
Ask me,
Ask me.

Well, I saw
A skeleton with no head,
On the bed of dread.
Ask me,
Ask me,
Ask me.

Well, I saw
The kite of night,
A skeleton with no head
On the bed of dread.
Ask me,
Ask me,
Ask me.

Well that is all I saw in the room of doom.

Shelley Francis (10)
Hornsea Community Primary School

Room 13 Poem

I went to a room.
It felt like doom.
What did I see?
Ask me,
Ask me,
Ask me.

Well I saw a
Skeleton without a head
Dancing on a bed.
What else did I see?
Ask me,
Ask me,
Ask me.

Well I saw an elf on a shelf
And a skeleton on a bed without a head.
What else did I see?
Ask me,
Ask me,
Ask me.

That's all I saw in room 13.

Haden Holmes (11)
Hornsea Community Primary School

My Room 13 Poem

I went to the room,
I was filled with gloom.
What did you see?
Ask me, ask me, ask me.

Well, I saw a skeleton with no head dancing on the bed.
What else did you see?
Ask me, ask me, ask me.

Well, I saw the bed of dread,
And a skeleton with no head dancing on the bed.
What else did you see?
Ask me, ask me, ask me.

Well I saw a rat with a hat,
And the bed of dread,
And a skeleton with no head dancing on the bed.
What else did you see?
Ask me, ask me, ask me.

Well I saw, a kite that gave me a fright,
And a rat with a hat,
And the bed of dread,
And a skeleton with no head dancing on the bed.
What else did you see?
Ask me, ask me, ask me.

Well I saw, the room of doom,
And a tomb,
And a kite that gave me a fright,
And Dracula's bite,
And a rat with a hat
That hit me with a bat,
And a skeleton with no head dancing on the bed

And that was all I saw when I went in the room!

Jessica Acklam (11)
Hornsea Community Primary School

Room 13

I went into the room,
And fell to my doom.
What did I see?
Ask me, ask me, ask me!
Well,
I saw a chained-up skeleton dangling from the roof.
What else did I see?
Ask me, ask me, ask me!
Well,
I saw a rat with a hat,
And an old stuffed bat,
And a chained-up skeleton dangling from the roof.
What else did I see?
Ask me, ask me, ask me!
Well,
I saw the bed of dread,
And a brain with no head,
And a rat with a hat,
And an old stuffed bat,
And a chained-up skeleton dangling from the roof.
What else did I see?
Ask me, ask me, ask me!
Well,
I saw the gate of fate,
And I ran off with my mate,
And the bed of dread,
And a brain with no head,
And a rat with a hat,
And an old stuffed bat,
And a chained-up skeleton dangling from the roof.
And that's all I saw in that hotel!

Mark Williams (11)
Hornsea Community Primary School

The Creepy Room 13

I went into the room,
I was filled with doom.
What did I see?
Guess,
Guess,
Guess.
Well I saw a skeleton without a head
jumping on the bed.
What else did I see?
Guess,
Guess,
Guess.
Well I saw the kite of night
and a skeleton jumping on the bed.
What else did I see?
Guess,
Guess,
Guess.
Well, I saw 192 stairs
and a man who said, 'Beware!',
the kite of night,
and a skeleton without a head,
and that's all I saw in room 13!

Zara-Faith Evans (10)
Hornsea Community Primary School

The Room 13 Poem!

I went to a spooky room
and saw a strange tomb.
What did I see?
Well, well, well,
a skeleton with no head dancing on the bed!
What else did I see?
Well, well, well,
the bed of dread
and a skeleton with no head dancing on the bed!
What else did I see?
Well, well, well,
the kite of fright in the middle of the night,
the bed of dread
and a skeleton with no head dancing on the bed!
What else did I see?
Well, well, well, the room of doom,
the kite of fright in the middle of the night,
the bed of dread
and a skeleton with no head dancing on the bed.

Jack Tonks (10)
Hornsea Community Primary School

My Playground

The silky cobwebs hang from trees.
The playground is deserted.
Somebody has vandalised it but no one's there.

I run to the swings.
I see small creatures dart under the trees.
A dust ball crawls across the playground.

There's a ghost in the playground.
I warn the children to stay away,
They don't listen, they just play.
Next I see it's back to normal.
I close my eyes, it's there again.

There's a broken fence vandalised by the ghost.
A tornado sweeps everything up.
My playground is dead!

Emma Pilling (10)
Longman's Hill CP School

Winter Days

It is snowing
Let's go out to play
Everyone's happy
Having a good day.

Throwing snowballs
In the snow
Come on, let's go

Building snowmen
With white snow
Here we go.

Patrick Gouldsbrough (10)
Longman's Hill CP School

The Unknown Garden

Sunlight beams on the unknown garden
Colourful arrows, swooping, gliding.

Beautiful butterflies,
Fly over a crystal clear lake,
Filled with golden darts swerving in and out.

Gigantic willows,
Swishing, swaying, in the delicate breeze.

Oval flowerbed covered in a rash of red poppies,
Red as fresh blood.

This is my garden, the secret garden!

Ben Pike (10)
Longman's Hill CP School

I Walked Along the Stream

I walked along the stream
Tropical fish swimming free
The piranhas swam to the sea
As I walked along the stream.

As I ran through the woods
I heard the beating of horses' feet
They galloped through the woods
As I ran through the woods

I stumbled along the road
As cars rumbled by
They rushed to and fro
As I stumbled along the road.

Angus Kirkby (10)
Longman's Hill CP School

The Workers

The workers work all day
but stop at night when I go to bed.
In the morning they go to the water tank,
but always when I'm in the bathroom!

After they've checked the pump,
the red liquid is tested.
When I go to school,
the workers go to HQ.

During my lunchtime,
the workers go to the barrel.
But what's going in it today?
Some vegetables they hope.

The supports of the factory
are rubbed with dairy products.
The crushers also.

So that is the factory,
marvellous and great.
The workers work all day,
but stop when I go to bed.

Jake Holliday (10)
Longman's Hill CP School

The Perfect Day

Sun coming up as slow as a snail
and sky as blue as the reef.

Chair lifts like electricity pylons
sweeping up and down.
Air blowing as cold
as an ice cube in a freezer
on a giant mountain.

Stuart Fox (11)
Longman's Hill CP School

Day And Night

Sunlight
Creeps sly as a fox.

Dew displayed
On grass.

Darts flashing past
Through sparkling water.

Darkness
Comes slow as a tortoise.

Owls come out
In the night sky breeze.

The moon is out
White like snow.

Liam O'Hara (10)
Longman's Hill CP School

Contrast

Winter days, dark, gloomy,
Snow melts in our hands,
All is frozen, no word is spoken,
All on this damp day.

Summer days, light, refreshing,
Ice cream melts in the beam,
The sun is nearer, the air is clearer,
All on this sunny day.

Josh Pike (10)
Longman's Hill CP School

Time, Precious Time

Time, precious time,
All the time in the world, yet none.

Time, tidy time.

Playing your favourite game,
tidy up

Time, teatime,
Eating your cooked dinner,
then it's cold

Time, precious time,
All the time in the world,
yet none!

Time, bedtime,
Brushing your teeth,
then morning .

Time, home time,
You only just get home,
then bed.

Time, wasted time.

Procrastination, then
time's gone

Time, fun time,
Playing with your friend,
then time's gone.

Time, precious time,
All the time in the world,
yet none!

Time, sad time,
When you're down at rock
bottom, dismal.

Time, playtime,
Playing tig, running,
time's gone.

Time, precious time,
All the time in the world, yet none.

Lewis Connell (11)
Longman's Hill CP School

I Saw It Out My Window

I saw it out my window,
The glittering sunlight shining,
Making the water shine like crystals.

There was a glimpse of a golden dart,
Firing through the water like a shining bullet.

The snoozing trees were spread around the stream,
With a blanket of leaves surrounding it.

I saw it out my window.

Oliver Bloxham (10)
Longman's Hill CP School

My Place

My place is like something revealed
The trees that sway in the breeze
Rabbits popping up to say hello
My lake as clear as diamonds
Grass covered in dew
Flower heads looking around, looking at me.
Stop, stand still.

My place is like something unrevealed
. The trees as still as a statue
Rabbits laying down their tired heads
My lake . . . as clear as diamonds
Grass covered in dew
Flower heads looking around, looking at me.
Night has fallen.

Georgia Southern (10)
Longman's Hill CP School

My Hiding Place

A blank place to hide,
No excitement inside.
You can hear me,
But not see.
This hiding place
Is for me.

The once so bright place,
Now dark and tired.
No growth for now,
All bare and unknown is my place.

Littered, polluted, so uncared for,
Neglected, neglected.
No place for me!

Kacey Sorby Richardson (11)
Longman's Hill CP School

Winter Warmer

I walked into a forest
and I heard the breeze
I heard a horse
galloping through the trees

Leaves fell from the branches
swish, swish!
I heard a tree swaying
while I was playing

Attention was around me
I saw a buzzy bee
I could see
a big brown tree

I walked into the forest
and I heard the breeze
I heard a horse
galloping through the trees.

Jack Noble (11)
Longman's Hill CP School

Vandals

It was a dark, dark night
And the vandals came out.
While everyone was at home,
They went to the park,
Killed the flowers,
Knocked down the climbing frame,
And sprayed the railway bridge.
It was a dark, dark night
And the vandals came out.
I wish they hadn't.

Mark Heslam (10)
Longman's Hill CP School

There's A Secret Garden

There's a secret garden
In my backyard.

Leaves floating down,
Like a shiny crown.

An old rusty gate,
Like a saint.

The sun creeps up
Behind the gate.

When you go in my secret garden you see,
Tropical trees blowing in the breeze
And buzzing bees.

There's a secret garden
In my backyard.

Jennifer Wilson (10)
Longman's Hill CP School

The Riverbank

Walking down the riverbank,
The sunrays aiming,
Blinding,
Trees,
Dragging,
Leaving behind twigs that fall,
People,
Children,
Collecting,
Reusing,
Moon comes up,
People gone,
No one to see,
Badgers,
Hedgehogs,
Coming out from the darkness of their dens.

Bethany Stephenson (11)
Longman's Hill CP School

Sliced

The beast awakes.
Swings his tail.
A sapling falls.
The monster . . .
Self-propels himself,
Over the lake.

The night sky.
Perfect cover.
The bone-crunching shadow,
Finds his prey.
A whip of his tail,
Slash
A bleeding corpse.

Morning . . .
A flash of light.
Brave warrior,
A vortex blade punctured,
The scales of the
Beast.
His head . . .
Sliced!

Tom Bruce (11)
Longman's Hill CP School

Fizz! Crash! Smash!

Fizz!
Snap!
Glass smashing to the floor!
Skin blue, purple, green.
Fire!
Steam sparkling
Off a mix
Of materials.

Crash!
Smash!
Containers
Flew to the floor.

Tick!
Tock!
The clock struck midnight,
And as it did
The life-saving
Red and yellow liquid
Was spilt.

Liam Golton (11)
Longman's Hill CP School

A Hiding Place

A hiding place nowhere to be seen
A hole for a mole in the ground
Trees going *whoosh, swoosh*
People sinking in the ground.

Fish wriggling in the water blowing bubbles
In and out of the rocks and darting through the plants
Swim, swim, swim, swim
Going to collect flakes of food.

A hiding place nowhere to be seen
From the moist, soft soil
A badger raises its head up and down
Looking to see if any danger's around.

A hiding place nowhere to be seen
A hole for a mole in the ground
Trees going *whoosh, swoosh*
People sinking in the ground.

Courtney Eleanor Render (10)
Longman's Hill CP School

Peace

Quiet
Waiting
Swirling track that's been drizzled
From a giant spoon.

Helpers arrive to dress the host
Banners, balloons and flags.

Quiet
Waiting
Vehicles roar like a lion.

Peace
Quiet.

Billy Glassby (11)
Longman's Hill CP School

My Hidey Home

Underneath the hedge,
Sunlight peeping through.
Pointy twigs digging into me,
But I don't care about anything in my hidey home.

I stare into the darkness,
That is all I do.
Every so often I sneak something to eat,
But nobody sees me in my hidey home.

I sit on the mud,
All day long.
When I get called, I don't go in,
When everybody is asleep I creep in.

Underneath the hedge,
Sunlight peeping through.
Pointy twigs digging into me
But I don't care about anything in my hidey home.

Grace Dowdy (10)
Longman's Hill CP School

The Farmyard

Light . . .
Horses' heads peeking from the stables
hens' beaks poking through the railings of the pen
a tractor starting up, heading for the barn
the farmhouse fire crackling
big fields stretching across the land
fences cutting in-between
mice running under broken tractors
cats snooping around by the pig huts
sheepdogs barking and charging after the sheep.

The sun goes down and melts away.

Evie Smyth (11)
Longman's Hill CP School

A Place Never Seen Before

The blossomed flowers stand swaying in the sun,
The wind tickles the back of your neck,
Hearing only the sound of your thoughts,
Going to a place never seen before.

A golden pathway that is never to end,
Stepping stones to never begin,
A palace that was never built,
In the place never seen before.

The ripe bushes swaying together,
The green tree fingers reaching down,
The pond dazzling in the breeze,
Going to a place never seen before.

Grass that is never to be cut,
The trees never to grow,
The flowers never to die,
In the place never seen before.

Lucy Crawford (9)
Longman's Hill CP School

Sunlight

Sunlight like a golden ball
Beautiful butterflies
Flying over a crystal-blue lake

Golden darts swishing in and out
The trees swaying in the breeze
The wind rustling
Sunlight, sunlight, sunlight.

Connor Mumby (11)
Longman's Hill CP School

The Signs Of Winter

Dark like black magic in a hole,
it is a snug small rodent which moves slowly.
What is it? A mole.

Crystal-like small dew on grass
swaying in the cold air breeze
also on some of the tallest trees.

Golden small creatures
darting out of the freezing water
and swimming about.

Orangey-red and sly as anything
but as fast as a fly
is the old withered fox.

Black and white with a tint of grey
grumpy,
lives in a bumpy burrow
and has no sorrow.

Sam Hawe (11)
Longman's Hill CP School

As I Look Through The Window

As I look from the window,
I see the sun creeping up.

The moonlight falling slowly,
Behind the hills.

Foxes wake and search for breakfast.
Hedgehogs hide away ready for the night.

A tweeting noise comes from the trees,
As I look from the window.

Matthew O'Connor (10)
Longman's Hill CP School

Ocean

The ocean.
Dark, light.
What does it look like?

A never-ending path.
Still.
Rocking in the wind.

Children laughing in your ears.
Adults talking.
Gossip.
Rumours.
Playing.
Having fun.

Down.
    Down.
        Down!

Fish swimming.
Red.
Yellow.
Orange.
Blue.

Coral.
Seaweed.

Colourful.

The ocean.
Dark, light.
Dark.

Settling for bed.

Calm, plain, still.
Alone.

We rest till morning.

Katie May Todd (11)
Longman's Hill CP School

Steaming, Streaming, Screaming.

The kettle,
Turning on
And turning off.
Whistling,
Steaming, streaming, screaming,
Through the day.

Changing colour
When it pours,
Adding things like sugar,
And milk.

Stirring,
And turning,
Round and
Round,
Whilst the grains
Dissolve into
Brown
Liquid.

Helping people,
Get through the day.
Cheering them up,
With every sip they take.

The kettle,
Turning on
And turning off.
Whistling.
Steaming, streaming, screaming
Through the day.

Ellis Piercy (11)
Longman's Hill CP School

The Sea

It stood there,
going back and forth.
Whish!
Wash!
Whoosh!
Went
the dark blue sea.

It stood there
falling to pieces.
Crash!
Hitting
the rocks below.

It stood there
waiting
for the call.
The boat
floating
on the sea's surface.

It stood there
going back and forth
Whish!
Wash!
Whoosh!
went
the dark blue sea.

Robert Howard (11)
Longman's Hill CP School

The Silver Moons

Full moon full of silver oceans
like a bowl of mushroom soup
being gulped down by the sky,
like a magical clock that doesn't go *tick-tock,*
by the light of which the owl travels.

Half moon, full banana,
like a lonely piece of orange,
like a football tucked half behind a turf of grass,
like the letter C floating around in loneliness
with only the stars for friends.

Jasmine Ruby Hale (9)
Sidmouth Primary School

The Full Moon

The full moon is like a yellow bouncy ball.
Like a silver piece of cheese.
Like a big eye winking gently at me.
Like a ball of gold shining glittery in the night.
Like the moon sparkling in the night.

The crescent moon is like a shivering glittery smile.
Like a half-bright light.
Like a colourful rainbow.
Like a sparkling lip.
Like a shivering half clock.

Alisha Freer (9)
Sidmouth Primary School

The Crescent And Full Moon

The crescent moon
is like a white, slightly shaded boomerang that's been catapulted
into the air and frozen,
like a shadowy spotty banana,
like a beautiful smile frozen forever.

The full moon
is like a frozen face smiling a beautiful smile forever,
is like a colossal football that's been kicked into outer space.

Lewis Alex Scott (8)
Sidmouth Primary School

The Night's Eye

The full moon is like a tiny shadow that follows you wherever you go,
like a huge white and grey patterned blob,
like a huge face with chickenpox.

The crescent moon is like a sparkling, beautiful crystal that has
been thrown into space,
like a piece of a star broken and left behind,
like a small piece of a broken seashell.

Molly Wagner (8)
Sidmouth Primary School

The Moon

The full moon is like a grey and white football soaring through the air.
Like some white cheese that you can reach out and grab.
Like a grey eye gazing at the world.

The crescent moon is like a smiling mouth with a gorgeous set
of white sparkling teeth.
Like a boomerang slowly bobbing around in the sky.
Like a piece of extremely spotty cheese.

Yasmin Malek (9)
Sidmouth Primary School

Pencils, Pencils

Pencils, pencils everywhere.
To throw them around I wouldn't dare.

Pencils, pencils on the page.
Don't go to the ice like the Ice Age.

Pencils, pencils, dozens of them.
Everybody will need a pen.

Ross Cudbertson (9)
Southcoates Primary School

Rabbits

R abbits are furry friends.
A rabbit needs love and care.
B ees can sting them.
B ees can harm them.
I think rabbits can run very fast.
T rees are their very shady home.
S ometimes they are really good friends.

Courtney Wilson (9)
Southcoates Primary School

I'm Not Going To School

I'm not going to school today
Just look at me, do I look OK?
I have got a terrible sprain
That makes me look like Mary Jane
It is painful having a horrible disease
It must have been that mouldy cheese
Look at me!
I have got chickenpox
As big as childish building blocks . . .

How do I feel today?
Much better, it is Saturday . . .

. . . Two days later . . .
Oh no, it is school today
I have got a horrible pain
Just look at my swollen eye
It must have been that disgusting pie
What? What's that you say?
It's teacher training day!
Bye-bye, I am off to play.

Saffie Pick (9)
Sutton Park Primary School

Young Writers Information

We hope you have enjoyed reading this book - and that you will continue to enjoy it in the coming years.

If you like reading and writing poetry drop us a line, or give us a call, and we'll send you a free information pack.

Alternatively if you would like to order further copies of this book or any of our other titles, then please give us a call or log onto our website at www.youngwriters.co.uk

Young Writers Information
Remus House
Coltsfoot Drive
Peterborough
PE2 9JX

(01733) 890066